do not know

95p

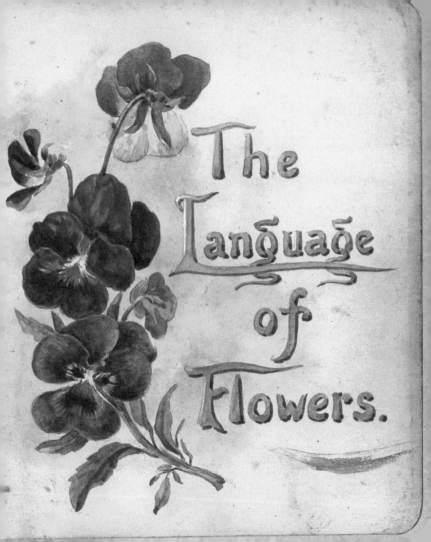

The Language of Flowers.

To Mother, Wishing you many happy returns of
the day. from Father
August 8th
19

There is a language, "little known",
Lovers claim it as their own.
Its symbols smile upon the land,
Wrought by Natures wonderous hand;
And in their silent beauty speak.
Of life and joy, to those who seek
For Love Divine and sunny hours
In the language of the flowers.

F.W.L.

Abatina	Fickleness.
Acacia	Chaste love.
Acacia, pink	Elegance.
Acacia, yellow	Secret love.
Acanthus	The Fine Arts. Artifice.
Achillea Millefolia	War.
Aconite, Wolfsbane	Misanthropy.
Aconite, Crowfoot	Lustre.
Adonis	Sorrowful remembrance.
African Marigold	Vulgar minds.
Agnus Castus	Coldness.
Agrimony	Thankfulness, Gratitude.
Almond	Stupidity. Indiscretion.
Almond, Flowering	Hope.
Almond, Laurel	Perfidy.
Allspice	Compassion.
Aloe	Grief, Affection.
Althæa Frutex	Persuasion
Alsysum, Sweet	Worth beyond beauty.
Amaranth	Immortality, Unfading love.
Amaranth, Globe	Unchangeable.
Amaranth, Cockscomb	Foppery, Affectation.
Amaryllis	Pride.
Ambrosia	Love returned.
American Elm	Patriotism.
American Linden	Matrimony.
American Starwort	Welcome to a stranger + Cheerfulness in old age.
Amethyst	Admiration.
Andromeda	Selfsacrifice.
Anemone, (Field)	Sickness

Anemone (Garden,	Forsaken.
Angelica,	Inspiration.
Angrec,	Royalty.
Apple,	Temptation
Apple Blossom,	Preference.
Apple, Thorn,	Deceitful Charms.
Apple, Pine,	Perfection.
Apocynum,	Deceit.
Arbor Vitæ,	Unchanging friendship.
Arum, Wake Robin	Ardour.
Ash-leaved Trumpet Flower,	Separation.
Ash, Mountain,	Prudence.
Ash Tree,	Grandeur.
Aspen Tree,	Lamentation.
Aster, China,	Variety.
Asphodel,	My regrets follow you to the grave
Auricula,	Painting.
Auricula, Green Edged	Importune me not.
Auricula, Scarlet	Avarice.
Azalea,	Temperance.
Azalea, Indian	True to the end.

B

Bachelor's Buttons,	Single blessedness.
Balm,	Sympathy.
Balm, Gentle,	Pleasantry.
Balm of Gilead	Cure. Releif.
Balsam,	Impatience.
Balsam, Red,	Touch me not. Impatient resol

Barberry,	Sourness, Sharpness. Ill temper.
Basil,	Hatred,
Bay Leaf,	I change but in death.
Bay Tree,	Glory.
Bay Wreath,	Reward of merit.
Bearded Crepis,	Protection.
Beech Tree,	Prosperity.
Bee Orchis,	Industry.
Bee Ophrys	Error.
Begonia	Dark Thoughts.
Belladonna	Silence.
Bell Flower, White	Gratitude.
Belvedere	I declare against you.
Betony,	Surprise.
Bilberry	Treachery.
Bindweed, Great	Insinuation.
Bindweed, small	Humility.
Birch	Meekness.
Birdsfoot Trefoil	Revenge.
Bittersweet; Nightshade	Truth.
Black Poplar,	Courage.
Black Thorne,	Difficulty.
Bladder Nut Tree	Frivolity. Amusement.
Bluebottle, Centaury	Delicacy.
Blue Bell,	Constancy.
Blue-flowered Greek Valerian,	Rupture.
Bonus Henricus	Goodness.
Borage,	Bluntness.
Box Tree,	Stoicism.
Bramble	Lowliness. Envy. Remorse.

Branch of Currants, ... You please all.
Branch of Thorns, ... Severity or Rigour.
Bridal Rose, ... Happy Love.
Broom, ... Neatness Humility.
Buckbean, ... Calm, Repose.
Bud of White Rose, ... A heart ignorant of love
Bugloss, ... Falsehood.
Butrush, ... Docility.
Bundle of Reeds, with
their panicles . . . . Music.
Burdock, ... Importunity. Touch me not
Buttercup, Kingcup. . . . . Childishness Ingratitude
Butterfly Orchis, ... Gaity.
Butterfly Weed, ... Let me go.

C   Cabbage, ... Profit.
    Cacalia, ... Adulation.
    Cactus, ... Warmth.
    Calla Æthiopica, ... Magnificent beauty.
    Calceolaria, ... Keep this for my sake.
    Calycanthus, ... Benevolence
    Camellia Japonica (Red WHITE. RED WHITE. Loveline ba
                                Unpretending excellence.
    Camomile, ... Energy in adversity.
    Companula or PYRAMIDAL BELL
                  flower. . . . Gratitude
    Canariensis, ... Self-esteem.
    Canary grass, ... Perseverance.
    Candytuft, ... Indifference.
    Canterbury Bell, ... Acknowledgment.
    Cardamine, ... Paternal error.
    Carnation, Red. . . . . . . Alas for my poor heart.

Carnation, Striped	Refusal.
Carnation, Yellow	Disdain.
Cardinal Flower	Distinction.
Catchfly,	Snare.
Catchfly, Red,	Youthful love.
Catchfly, White,	Betrayed.
Cedar,	Strength.
Cedar of Lebanon,	Incorruptible.
Cedar Leaf,	I live for thee.
Celandine,	Joys to come.
Cerehus, Creeping	Modest Genius.
Centuary,	Felicity.
Champignon,	Suspicion.
Checquered, Fritillary	Persecution.
Cherry Tree,	Good education.
Cherry Tree (Winter),	Deception.
Chestnut,	Luxury.
Chestnut Tree,	Do me justice.
Chickweed,	Rendezvous.
Chicory,	Frugality.
China Aster,	Variety.
China Aster, Double	I partake your sentiments.
China Aster, Single	I will think of it.
China Rose,	Beauty always new.
Chinese Chrysanthemum	Cheefulness under adversity.
Christmas Rose,	Relieve my anxiety.
Chrysanthemum, Red	I love.
Chrysanthemum, Yellow	Slighted love.
Chrysanthemum, White,	Truth.
Cineraria,	Ever bright.

Cinquefoil,	Maternal affection.
Circæa,	Spell.
Cistus or Rock Rose,	Popular favour.
Cistus Gum,	I shall die tomorrow.
Citron,	Beauty with ill-humour.
Clarkia	Will you dance with me
Clematis	Mental beauty.
Clematis, Evergreen,	Poverty.
Cloves,	Dignity.
Clover, Four-leaved,	Be mine.
Clover, red,	Industry.
Clover, White,	Think of me.
Cobœa,	Gossip.
Cockscomb Amaranth	Singularity.
Colchicum, or Meadow Saffron	~~Justice~~ My best days are pas
Coltsfoot,	Justice shall be done
Columbine,	Folly.
Columbine, Purple	Resolution.
Columbine, Red	Anxious and Trembling
Convolvulus,	Bonds. Uncertainty.
Convolvulus, Minor,	Night.
Convolvulus, Major,	Extinguished hopes.
Convolvulus, Pink,	Worth sustained by judicious and tender affection
Corchorus,	Impatient of absence.
Coreopsis,	Always cheerful.
Coreopsis, Arkansa	Love at first sight.
Coriander,	Concealed merit.
Corn,	Riches.
Corn, Broken,	Quarrel.

Corn Straw,	Agreement,
Corn Bottle,	Delicacy,
Corn Cockle,	Duration, Gentility
Coronella,	Success crown your wishes
Cornel Tree,	Duration.
Cowslip,	Pensiveness, Winning grace
Cowslip, American,	You are my divinity.
Crab Blossom,	Ill nature.
Cranberry,	Hardness.
Creeping Cereus,	Horror.
Cress,	Stability.
Crocus,	Abuse not.
Crocus, Spring	Youthful gladness.
Crocus, Saffron	Mirth.
Crown, Imperial	Majesty. Power.
Crownbill,	Envy.
Crows foot,	Ingratitude.
Cuckoo Pint,	Ardour.
Cudweed,	Never ceasing remembrance
Currants,	You please all.
Cuscuta,	Meanness.
Cyclamen,	Diffidence.
Cypress,	Death, Despair, Mourning,
Daffodil,	Regard.
Daffodil, Great yellow	Chivalry.
Dahlia, Single	Good taste.
Dahlia,	Instability.
Daisy, Double	Participation.

Daisy, Garden,	I share your sentiment
Daisy, Ox Eye,	A Token.
Daisy, Party Coloured	Beauty.
Daisy, Red,	Unconscious.
Daisy, White,	Innocence.
Daisy, Wild,	I will think of it.
Dandelion,	Oracle.
Daphne Odora,	Painting the Lily
Darnel,	Vice.
Dead Leaves,	Sadness.
Dew Plant,	A serenade.
Diosma,	Uselenness,
Dittany of Crete,	Birth,
Dittany, White,	Passion.
Dock,	Patience.
Dodder of Thyme	Baseness,
Dogsbane,	Deceit Falsehood.
Dogwood,	Durability.
Dragon Plant,	Snare,
Dragonwort.	Horror.
Dried Flax	Utility.

E

Ebony Tree,	Blackness.
Eglantine or Sweet Briar	Poetry ... I wound to heal.
Elder,	Zealousness.
Elm,	Dignity.

Enchanter's Nightshade,	Fascination. Witchcraft.
Endive,	Frugality.
Eschscholtzia,	Sweetness
Eupatorium,	Delay.
Evergreen,	Poverty.
Evergreen, Thorn,	Solace in Adversity.
Everlasting Pea,	Lasting pleasure and an appointed meeting.
Fennel,	Worthy of all praise.
Fern, Flowering,	Fascination.
Fern,	Sincerity.
Ficoides, Ice Plant,	Your looks freeze me.
Fig,	Argument.
Fig, Marigold,	Idleness.
Fig, Tree,	Prolific.
Flax, Fate,	Domestic industry. I feel your kindness.
Flax-leaved Golden Locks,	Tardiness.
Fleur-de-Lis,	Flame.
Fleur-de-Luce,	Fire.
Flowering Reed,	Confidence in heaven.
Flower-of-an-Hour,	Delicate beauty.
Fly Orchis,	Error.
Fly Trap,	Deceit.
Fools Parsley,	Silliness,
Forget-me-Not	True love

F

Foxglove,	Insincerity.
Foxtail Grass,	Sporting.
French Honeysuckle,	Rustic Beauty.
French Marigold,	Jealousy
French Willow,	Bravery & Humanity
Frog Ophrys,	Disgust.
Fritillary, Chequered	Persecution.
Fullers. Teasel,	Misanthropy. Importunity.
Fumitory,	Spleen.
Fuchsia, Scarlet,	Taste.
Furze or Gorse,	Enduring affection.
Garden Anemone,	Forsaken.
Garden Chervil,	Sincerity,
Garden Marigold,	Uneasiness.
Garden Ranunculus,	You are rich in attractions.
Garden Sage,	Esteem.
Garland of Roses,	Reward of Virtue.
Gentian,	You are unjust.
Germander Speedwell,	Facility.
Geranium, Dark,	Melancholy,
Geranium, Ivy,	Bridal Favour,
Geranium, Nutmeg,	An expected meeting.
Geranium, Oak-leaved,	True friendship.
Geranium, Pencil-leaved,	Ingenuity,
Geranium, Rose or Pink,	Preference.
Geranium, Scarlet,	Comforting.

Geranium, Silvered leaved, ... Recall.
Geranium, Wild, ... Steadfast Piety.
Gilliflower, ... Lasting beauty,
Bonds of affection.
Gladiolus, ... Strength of Character.
Glory Flower, ... Glorious beauty,
Gloxinia, ... A proud Spirit.
Goats Rue, ... Reason.
Golden Rod, ... — Precaution, Encouragement.
Gooseberry, ... Anticipation.
Gourd, ... Extent. Bulk.
Grass, ... Utility. Submission.
Grape, Wild, ... Charity.
Guelder. Rose, ... Winter or Age.
Hand Flower Tree, ... Warning.
Harebell, ... Submission. Grief.
Hawkweed, ... Quick-sightedness.
Hawthorne, ... Hope:
Hazel, ... Reconciliation,
Heartsease or Pansy, ... You occupy my thoughts.
Heath, ... Solitude,
Helenium, ... Tears.
Heliotrope, ... Devotion.
Hellebore, ... Scandal. Calumny.
Hemlock, ... You will be my death.
Hemp, ... Fate.
Henbane, ... Imperfection.

Hepatica,	Confidence.
Hibiscus,	Delicate beauty.
Holly,	Foresight.
Holly Herb,	Enchantment.
Hollyhock,	Fecundity.
Honesty,	Honesty. Sincerity.
Honey, Flower,	Love sweet & secret.
Honeysuckle,	Bonds of Love sweetness of disposition.
Honeysuckle, Coral,	The color of my Fate.
Honeysuckle, French,	Rustic Beauty.
Hop,	Injustice.
Hornbeam	Ornament.
Hortensia,	You are cold.
Houseleek,	Vivacity, Domestic economy.
Houstonia,	Content,
Hoya,	Sculpture.
Humble Plant,	Despotism.
Hyacinth,	Sport, Game, Play.
Hyacinth, Purple,	Sorrow.
Hyacinth, Blue,	Constancy,
Hyacinth, White,	Unobtrusiveness loveliness.
Hydrangea,	A boaster, Heartlessness.
Hyssop,	Cleanliness.

I	Iceland Moss, ...	Health.
	Ice, Plant, ...	Your looks freeze me.
	Imperial Montague, ...	Power.
	Indian Cress, ...	Warlike trophy.
	Indian Pink, Double	Always Lovely.
	Indian Plum, ...	Privation.
	Iris, ...	Message,
	Iris, German, ...	Flame.
	Ivy, ...	Friendship, Fidelity, Marriage
	Ivy, sprig of with tendrils	Assiduous to please.
J	Jacobs Ladder, ...	Come down.
	Japan Rose, ...	Beauty is your only attraction.
	Jasmine, White, ...	Amiability.
	Jasmine, Cape, ...	Transport of joy.
	Jasmine, Carolina, ...	Separation.
	Jasmine, Indian, ...	Attachment.
	Jasmine, Spanish, ...	Sensuality.
	Jasmine, Yellow, ...	Grace and elegance.
	Jonquil, ...	I desire a return of affection.
	Judas, Tree, ...	Unbelief. Betrayal.
	Juniper, ...	Succour, Protection,
	Justicia, ...	The perfection of female loveliness
K	Kennedya, ...	Mental beauty.
L	King-Cups, ...	Desire of riches.
	Laburnum, ...	Forsaken, Pensive Beauty.

Lady's Slipper,	. . . .	Capricious beauty.
Lagerströmia, Indian,	. . .	Eloquence.
Lantana,	. . . .	Rigour.
Larch,	. . . .	Audacity, Boldness.
Larkspur,	. . . .	Lightness, Levity.
Larkspur, Pink,	. . . .	Fickleness.
Larkspur, Purple,	. . . . .	Haughtiness.
Laurel,	. . . .	Glory.
Laurel, Common, in flower	. .	Perfidy.
Laurel, Ground,	. . . . . .	Perseverance.
Laurel, Mountain,	. . . .	Ambition.
Laurestina,	. . . .	A Token.
Lavender,	. . . .	Distrust.
Leaves, Dead,	. . . . . .	Melancholy.
Lemon,	. . . .	Zest.
Lemon Blossoms,	. . . .	Fidelity in love.
Lent Lilly,	. . . . . .	Sweet disposition.
Lettuce,	. . . . .	Cold-heartedness.
Lichen,	. . . .	Dejection, Solitude.
Lilac, Field,	. . . . . .	Humility
Lilac, Purple,	. . . . . .	First emotions of love.
Lilac, White,	. . . . .	Youthful innocense.
Lily, Day,	. . . . . .	Coquetry.
Lily, Yellow,	. . . . . .	Falsehood, Gaiety.

Lilly of the Valley	Return of happiness.
Linden or Lime Tree,	Conjugal love.
Lint,	I feel my obligation.
Live Oak,	Liberty.
Liverwort,	Confidence.
Liquorice, Wild,	I declare against you
Lobelia,	Malevolence.
Locust Tree,	Elegance.
Locust Tree, Green	Affection beyond the grave.
London Pride,	Frivolity.
Lote Tree,	Concord.
Lotus,	Eloquence.
Lotus Flower,	Estranged love.
Lotus Leaf,	Recantation.
Love-in-a-mist,	Perplexity.
Love-lies-bleeding,	Hopeless, not heartless.
Lucerne,	Life.
Lupin,	Voraciousness.
Madder,	Calumny.
Magnolia,	Love of nature.
Magnolia, Laurel-leaved	Dignity.
Magnolia, Swamp,	Perseverance.
Mallow,	Mildness.
Mallow, Marsh,	Beneficence.
Mallow, Syrian,	Consumed by love
Mallow, Venetian,	Delicate Beauty.

M

Manchineel Tree,	Falsehood
Mandrake,	Horror.
Maple,	Reserve.
Marigold,	Grief. Despair.
Marigold, African,	Vulgar minds.
Marigold, French,	Jealousy.
Marigold, Prophetic,	Prediction.
Marjoram,	Blushes.
Marvel of Peru,	Timidity.
Meadow Lychnis,	Wit.
Meadow Saffron,	My best days are past.
Meadowsweet,	Uselessness.
Mercury,	Goodness.
Mesembryanthemum,	Idleness.
Mezereon,	Desire to please.
Michaelmas Daisy,	Afterthought.
Mignonette,	Your qualities surpass your charms
Milfoil,	War.
Milk vetch,	Your presence softens my pain
Milk wort,	Hermitage
Mimosa, Sensitive Plant,	Sensitiveness.
Mint,	Virtue,
Mistletoe,	I surmount difficulties.
Mock Orange,	Counterfeit.
Monkshood, Helmet flower,	Chivalry, Knight-errantry.
Moonwort,	Forgetfulness
Morning Glory,	Affectation,
Moschatel,	Weakness.
Moss,	Maternal love.

Mosses,	Ennui.
Mossy Saxifrage	Affection.
Motherwort,	Concealed love.
Mountain Ash,	Prudence.
Mourning Bride,	Unfortunate attachment. I have
Mouse-eared Chickweed,	Ingenuous simplicity.
Mouse-eared Scorpion Grass,	Forget me not.
Moving Plant,	Agitation.
Mudwort,	Happiness, Tranquillity.
Mulberry, Tree. Black	I shall not survive you.
Mulberry Tree White,	Wisdom.
Mushroom,	Suspicion.
Musk Plant,	Weakness.
Mustard Seed,	Indifference.
Myrobalan,	Privation.
Myrrh,	Gladness.
Myrtle,	Love.
Narcissus,	Egotism.
Narcissus, Double,	Feamale ambition.
Nasturtium,	Patriotism.
Nemophila,	I forgive you.
Nettle, Common stinging,	You are cruel.
Nettle, burning,	Slander.
Nettle Tree,	Conceit.
Night-blooming Cereus,	Transient beauty.
Night Convolvulus,	Night.
Nightshade,	Falsehood.
Oak Leaves,	Bravery.
Oak Tree,	Hospitality.

lost all.

Oak, White,	Independence.
Oats,	The witching soul of music.
Oleander,	Beware.
Olive,	Peace.
Orange blossoms,	Bridal festivities; and your purity equals your loveliness.
Orange flowers,	Chastity.
Orange Tree,	Generosity.
Orchis,	A belle.
Osier,	Frankness.
Osmunda,	Dreams.
Ox Eye,	Patience.
Palm,	Victory.
Pansy,	Thoughts.
Parsley,	Festivity.
Pasque Flower,	You have no claims.
Patience Dock,	Patience.
Passion Flower,	Religious superstition.
Pea, Everlasting,	An appointed meeting; lasting pleasure.
Pea, Sweet,	Departure + lasting pleasures.
Peach,	Your qualities like your charms are unequalled.
Peach Blossom,	I am your captive.
Pears,	Affection.
Pear Tree,	Comfort.
Pelargonium,	Eagerness.
Pelargonium, White,	Gracefulness.
Pelargonium, Red,	Her smile the soul of witchery.
Pentstemon,	Pleasure without alloy.
Pennyroyal,	Flee away.
Peony,	Shame bashfulness.
Peppermint,	Warmth of feeling.

Periwinkle, Blue,	Early friendship.
Periwinkle, White,	Pleasures of memory.
Persicaria,	Restoration.
Persimmon,	Bury me amid natures beauties
Peruvian Heliotroupe,	Devotion.
Petunia,	Never Despair.
Pheasant's Eye,	Remembrance.
Phlox,	Unanimity,
Pigeon Berry,	Indifference.
Pimpernel,	Change. Assignation
Pine,	Pity.
Pine-Apple,	You are perfect.
Pine, Pitch,	Philosophy.
Pine, Spruce,	Hope in adversity.
Pink,	Boldness.
Pink, Carnation,	Womans love.
Pink, Indian, Double,	Always lovely
Pink, Indian, Single,	Aversion.
Pink, Mountain,	Aspiring.
Pink, Red, Double,	Pure and ardent love.
Pink, Single,	Pure love.
Pink, Variegated,	Refusal.
Pink, White,	Ingeniousness, Talent.
Plane, Tree,	Genius.
Plum, Indian,	Privation.
Plum Tree,	Fidelity.
Plum, Wild,	Independence.
Polyanthus,	Pride of riches.
Polyanthus, Crimson,	The heart's mystery.
Polyanthus, Lilac,	Confidence.

Pomegranate, ... Foolishness.
Pomegranate Flower . . . . . Mature elegance.
Poplar, Black, ... Courage
Poplar, White, ... Time.
Poppy, Oriental, ... Silence,
Poppy, Red, ... Consolation
Poppy, Scarlet, ... Fantastic extravagance.
Poppy, White, ... Sleep - My bane.
Potatoe, ... Benevolence.
Prickley Pear, ... Satire.
Pride of China, ... Dissension.
Primrose, ... Early youth or sadness.
Primrose, Evening, ... Inconstancy.
Primula, ... Diffidence.
Privit, ... Prohibition.
Purple clover, ... Provident.
Pyrethrum, ... I am not changed, They wrong me.
Pyrus, Japonica, ... Faries fire.
Quaking Grass, ... Agitation.
Quamoclit, ... Busybody.
Queen's Rocket, ... You are the Queen of Coquettes ^Passion
Quince, ... Temptation.
Ragged Robbin . . . . Wit.
Ranunculus, ... You are radient with charms.
Ranunculus, Garden, ... You are rich in attractions.
Ranunculus, Wild, ... Ingratitude.
Raspberry, ... Remorse.
Rye Grass, Darnel, ... Vice.
Red Catchfly, ... Youthful love.

Q

R

Reed,	Complaisance, Music.
Reed Split,	Indiscretion.
Rhododendron, Rosebay,	Danger. Beware.
Rhubarb,	Advice.
Rocket,	Rivalry.
Rose,	Love.
Rose, Austrian,	Thou art all that is lovely.
Rose, Boule de Neige,	Only for thee.
Rose, Bridal,	Happy love.
Rose, Burgundy,	Unconscious beauty.
Rose, Cabbage,	Ambassador of love.
Rose, Campion,	Only deserve my love.
Rose, Carolina,	Love is dangerous.
Rose, Charles le fievree,	Speak low if you speak love.
Rose, China,	Beauty always new.
Rose, Christmas,	Relieve my anxiety.
Rose, Daily,	Thy smile I aspire to.
Rose, Damask,	Brilliant Complexion.
Rose, Deep Red,	Bashful shame.
Rose, Dog,	Pleasure and pain.
Rose, Gloire de Dijon,	A messenger of love.
Rose, Guelder,	Winter. Age.
Rose, Hundred-leaved,	Pride
Rose, Japan,	Beauty is your only attraction.
Rose, John Hopper,	Encouragement.
Rose, La France,	Meet me by moonlight.
Rose, Maiden Blush,	If you love me you will find it out
Rose, Monteflora,	Grace.
Rose, Mundi,	Variety.
Rose, Musk,	Capricious beauty.

Rose, Musk, Cluster, ... Charming.
Rose, Nephitos, ... Infatuation.
Rose, Single, ... Simplicity
Rose, Thornless, ... Early attachment.
Rose, Unique, ... Call me not beautiful.
Rose, White, ... I am worthy of you.
Rose, White (Withered) . . . . . . Transient impressions
Rose, Yellow, ... Decrease of love, Jealousy.
Rose, York & Lancaster, ... War.
Rose, Full-blown, placed over two buds . . . . Secrecy.
Rose, White & Red together, ... Unity.
Roses, Crown of, ... Reward of virtue.
Rosebud, Red, ... Pure and lovely
Rosebud, White, ... Girlhood & a heart ignorant of love
Rosebud, Moss, ... Confession of love.
Rosemary, ... Remembrance.
Rudbeckia, ... Justice.
Rue, ... Disdain.
Rush, ... Docilily.
Rye Grass, ... Changeable disposition.
Saffron, ... Beware of success,
Saffron, Crocus, ... Mirth.
Saffron, Meadow, ... My happiest days are past
Sage, ... Domestic virtue.
Sage, Garden, ... Esteem
Sainfoin, ... Agitation.
Saint John's Wort, ... Animosity.
Salvia, Blue, ... I think of you.
Salvia, Red, ... For ever thine.
Saxifrage, Mossy . . . . Affection.
Scabious, ... Unfortunate love.

Scarlet, Lychnis,	Sunbeaming eyes.
Schinus,	Religious enthusiasm.
Scilla, Blue,	Forgive & forget.
Scilla, Sibirica,	Pleasure without alloy.
Scilla, White,	Sweet innocence
Scotch, Fir,	Elevation.
Sensitive Plant,	Sensibility.
Shamrock,	Light-heartedness
Snakesfoot,	Horror.
Snowdragon,	Presumption
Snowball,	Bound.
Snowdrop,	Hope.
Sorrel,	Affection.
Sorrel, Wild,	Wit-ill timed.
Sorrel, Wood,	Joy.
Southernwood,	Jest. Bantering.
Spanish Jasmine,	Sensuality.
Spearmint,	Warmth of sentiment
Speedwell,	Female fidelity.
Speedwell. Germander,	Facility.
Speedwell, Spiked,	Semblance
Spider, Ophrys,	Adroitness.
NOTE ONE WORD Spider, Wort,	Esteem not love
Spiked, Willow Herb	Pretension.
Spindle Tree,	Your charms are engraven on my heart.
Star of Bethlehem,	Purity.
Starwort,	Afterthought.
Starwort, American,	Cheerfulness in old age.
Stephanotis,	You can boast too much.
Stock,	Lasting beauty.
Stock, Ten-week,	Promptness.

Stonecrop,	Tranquility.
Straw, Broken,	Rupture of a contract.
Straw, Whole,	Union.
Strawberry Blossoms	Foresight.
Strawberry Tree,	Esteem not love.
Sumach, Venice,	Splendour.
Sunflower, Dwarf,	Adoration.
Sunflower, Tall,	Haughtiness.
Swallow-wort,	Cure for heartache.
Sweet Basil,	Good wishes.
Sweetbriar, American,	Simplicity.
Sweetbriar, European,	I wound to heal.
Sweetbriar, Yellow,	Decrease of love.
Sweet Pea,	Delicate pleasures and departure.
Sweet Sultan,	Felicity.
Sweet William,	Gallantry.
Sycamore,	Curiosity.
Syringa,	Memory.
Syringa, Carolina,	Disappointment.
Tamarisk,	Crime.
Tansy, Wild,	I declare war against you.
Teasel,	Misanthropy.
Teasel, Fuller's,	Misanthropy.
Tendrils of climbing plants,	Ties.
Thistle, common,	Austerity.
Thistle, Scotch,	Retaliation.
Thorn, Apple,	Deceitful charms.
Thorns, Branch of,	Severity.
Thrift,	Sympathy.
Throatwort,	Neglected beauty.

Thyme,	Activity.
Tiger flower,	For once may pride befriend me
Traveller's Joy,	Safety.
Tree of Life,	Old age.
Trefoil,	Revenge,
Tremella Nestoc,	Resistance,
Trillium Pictum,	Modest beauty.
Truffle,	Surprise.
Trumpet Flower,	Fame.
Tuberose,	Dangerous pleasures.
Tulip, Red,	Declaration of love.
Tulip, Variegated,	Beautiful eyes.
Tulip, Yellow,	Hopeless love.
Turnip,	Charity.
Jussilago, Sweet-scented,	Justice shall be done you.
Valerian,	An accommodating disposition
Valerian, Greek,	Rupture.
Venice Sumach,	Intellectual excellence.
Venus's Car,	Fly with me.
Venus's Lookinglass,	Flattery.
Venus's Trap,	Deceit.
Verbena, Scarlet,	Sensibility,
Verbena, White,	Pure and Guileless.

Vernal Grass, ... Poor but happy.

Veronica, ... Fidelity.

Vervain, ... Enchantment.

Vine, ... — Intoxication.

Violet, Blue, ... Faithfulness.

Violet, Dame, ... Watchfulness.

Violet, Sweet, ... Modesty.

Violet Yellow, ... — Rural happiness.

Virginia Creeper, ... Ever Changing.

Virgin's Bower, ... Filial love.

Volkmannia, ... — — May you be happy.

Wallnut, ... Intellect . Stratagem.

Wall-Flower, ... Fidelity in Adversity.

Water Lily, ... Purity of heart.

Water Melon, ... Bulkiness.

Wax Plant, ... Susceptibility.

Weigela, ... Accept a faithful heart.

Wheat Stalk, ... Riches.

Whin, ... Anger.

White Jasmine, ... Amiability.

White Lily,	Purity and modesty.
White Mullein,	Good nature.
White Oak,	Independence.
White Pink,	Talent.
White Poplar,	Time.
Whortleberry,	Treason.
Willow, Creeping,	Love forsaken,
Willow, Water,	Freedom,
Willow, Weeping,	Mourning.
Willow, Herb,	Pretension.
Willow, French,	Bravery and Humanity.
Wistaria,	I cling to thee.
Witch Hazel,	A spell.
Woodbine,	Fraternal love.
Wood Sorrel,	Joy. Maternal tenderness.
Wormwood,	Absence.
Xanthium,	Rudeness. Pertinacity.
Xeranthemum,	Cheerfulness under adversity.
Yew,	Sorrow.
Zephyr Flower,	Expectation.
Zinnia,	Thoughts of absent friends.

~ *FINIS* ~.

First published in Great Britain
by Michael Joseph Ltd, 52 Bedford Square
London WC1 October 1968

Second Impression January 1971

Third Impression March 1974

Fourth Impression January 1976

ISBN 0 7181 0593 1

Printed by Beric Press Ltd, Crawley